How To Sell Any Product Online

"Secrets of The Killer Sales Letter"

Omar Johnson

Table of Contents

Introduction

Whether you are just getting into creating a home-based business or you are an experienced marketer, you've probably seen the same sites on the Internet. Sites that promise you the secrets of creating killer sales copy, or how to write the sales page that will make you millions.

The truth is that a lot of these sites offer the same generic advice and the same generic form letters that won't help you make sales. What sells on the Internet is passion and words that captivate consumers in such a way that they will be forking over their credit cards in no time.

With this sales manual, you will learn the basics of selling on the Web, get an overview of marketing basics, and learn how to craft a sales letter that really sells.

We'll start off by getting to know your customer. Who are they? How much money do they have? How do they think?

Then, we'll look at your products and services from a customer's point of view. What makes your product different from the rest? Why should a person buy your product instead of your competitors?

Then, we'll explore the various things you will use to write your sales letter, from basic copywriting tips, to works that sell, to creating snappy headlines.

And finally, we'll offer you a couple of tips that the pros use that will really get your sales going!

Chapter 1: Creating a Customer Profile

The most important thing for any marketing effort is to make sure you have a target audience identified. By targeting a specific niche group, you will be giving yourself a valuable insight into the mind of your consumer.

The more you know your audience, the easier it will be to sell them your products by tailoring your marketing to their needs.

In addition, you'll be saving your business money, because marketing to a mass audience is much more expensive than marketing to a small segment of the population.

Creating a customer profile will help you:

- Make better decisions about how to spend your marketing dollars.

- Pinpoint the exact kind of services and products that will attract a particular customer.
- Minimize mistakes caused by not knowing your customer base.

Your Customer at a Glance

There are two ways that you can create a customer profile using demographics and/or psychographics.

With demographics, you create a customer profile based on some of the following variables: age, gender, income level, marital status, location, occupation, education level, etc.

By identifying your customer in this way, you are both defining markets for your products or services and giving yourself a tool to use when the marketplace starts to change.

For example, I want to sell kits to stay-at-home moms that will help them launch a crafts business. So I would start with a demographic profile of the kind of customer I want to come to my Web site. Let's call her Susie.

Susie is a 32-year-old woman who is married and stays at home with her kids, ages 5 and 8. Her husband makes at least $50,000 per year, and Susie has earned at least an associate's degree from a college.

Now, remember this demographic information, and we'll come back to it.

Now you'll make a psychographics profile of Susie. Psychographics shows you why your customers behave the way they do.

Customer behavior is a very strong predictor of sales, and used in conjunction with a demographic profile, you will have a great start in defining your target audience. Also, you will be able to gain valuable insights into how to market your product through this kind of profile.

Psychographics include how your customer decides to buy a product (price point, quality, service, etc.), how often your customer will buy your product, the need your product will fill for a customer, and how they currently fill that need.

So here's Susie, again:

Demographic: Susie is a 32-year-old woman who is married and stays at home with her kids, ages 5 and 8. Her husband makes at least $50,000 per year, and Susie has earned at least an associate's degree from a college.

Psychographic: Since Susie is in a family with only one income, she will be attracted to something that will help her launch a home-based business. Her husband makes enough money to make the family middle class, but not so much that she will be have thousands of dollars at her disposal to launch this business. She will likely only purchase your product once.

With this analysis, you've learned several things. First, your price point can't be too high, because your customers come from one-income families.

Second, you've learned that with your current product a home-business start-up kit will only give a customer the opportunity to purchase from you once.

Constantly capturing and converting new customers can be an expensive proposition. With this information, you may also want to add ancillary products and services, such as business counseling or coaching, other kits, etc. That way, you can get Susie to purchase from you several times.

The Details

How detailed should your customer
profile be? That depends on how big
your target audience is going to
be. You can certainly have more
than one kind of customer profile.
This will help you market to
different population segments and
diversify your revenue streams. You
can also create profiles for each
product line or for each specific
product.

You should also do some market
research before you create your
customer profile. You can have
conversations with potential
customers or look up third-party
research articles and reports. The
point is to get as much information
as possible before creating your
profile.

Even so, you're probably going to
have to fill in some gaps in your
profile through guess-work. You
might have to come up with a

generic age range that can be further refined once you have some customers to work with.

I Have a Profile. Now What?

We've just created a profile for prospective customers. With this, you can prepare your marketing and communications plan. You can use this profile with both direct and indirect marketing. Use your profile to decide where and how to advertise. Offer specials and discounts based on what you've learned.

Once you have launched your Web site and have a range of customers to profile, you can start gaining knowledge to add to these profiles, such as buying habits, through the use of purchase tracking, surveys, and more. This existing-customer profile can be used to try and increase your per-customer revenue average, etc.

Make sure that you review and add to your profile regularly. Markets change and people's buying habits change.

As that happens, your customer profiles should naturally change, and you may have to change your marketing options as well.

Chapter 2: What Makes Your Product Different?

Creating a Unique Selling Position

Once you've chosen your target audience, you need to create a unique selling position (USP) for your product. This will tell your customers why your product is different from your competitor's.

When a customer is looking to purchase something, the first thing they think is, "What's in it for me? If I buy your product, instead of Joe's, what do I get in return?"

Showcase how you are different than the competition. And we're not talking about generalities that any business can claim.

Take a look at mattress commercials on TV. All claim to have the lowest prices, the best deals, etc. Well, if you were going into the mattress-selling business, wouldn't you want to present yourself differently?

Maybe you would want to focus on the quality of your products or a replacement guarantee.

You need to figure out what gives you a unique advantage over your competition. Why will your customers buy from you? What can you provide to customers that no other business can?

Step 1: Know Your Competition

Before you can create your unique selling position, you need to see what the competition is doing.

Start your competitive analysis by identifying the leading companies in your industry. The Web often makes this easy to do, but what if you can't seem to find any major competitors just by searching through Google?

You might need to pick up a phone book and take a look at the ads, or

14

search through back issues of local business journals if your competitors are based locally.

If your competitors are all over the U.S., then you will have to be a little more creative. Look at advertisements on major Web sites, listings in directories, etc.

Once you have the leaders pinpointed, map out what you know about them. Can you figure out a way to get more information, perhaps posing as a customer to see how they sell to prospects? Can you figure out which companies are the biggest threats to your business?

Step 2: Know Your Product

It's important to consider what's called the "4 P's" of marketing – pricing, product, promotion, and place. This is also known as the marketing mix, as it is a combination of these items that will help you create your USP.

So, if you are going to highlight price in your USP, remember what motivates your customer's behavior. Don't just say you have the lowest prices; explain why. If you have a one-of-a-kind product, explain to your customer why the price reflects this.

Price is almost never the only reason that people will buy a product, so you will also need to add something else into the mix:

Product: What are you selling? Are you taking a common item and packaging it in a new way?

A very famous story about this "P" is how Hanes L'Eggs pantyhose came to be packaged in its unique egg shape.

Stockings and pantyhose used to be sold only through department stores. Hanes decided to open a new distribution channel in grocery stores, by packaging this as a consumer staple – along with milk, cheese, and, of course, regular eggs. They decided to package the hosiery so that it would fit in with groceries, hence the "egg."

Promotion: Good promotion will compel your customers to purchase your product. Can you tie a sale or other promotion to a particular geographic location, or holiday, or time of year?

Place (distribution): Can you get the right product to the right person at the right time? This increases customer satisfaction and hikes up your sales numbers.

Step 3: Tie It All Together

Keep in mind your customer profile while creating your USP, because it is very expensive and time-consuming to convince a customer to buy something that he or she doesn't want or need.

Now you have a lot of valuable information: who your customers are (customer profile), what your competition is doing, and what is interesting about your product. With this you can begin to construct your USP.

Your USP should be very simple; one sentence that is believable and that clearly illustrates a unique benefit that a customer will get from your product. "Buy this product, and you will get this specific benefit."

Here are some national product's USP:

Red Bull: Gives you energy

Oil of Olay: Gives you younger looking skin

Dell: Takes the hassle out of buying a computer

Chapter 3: Storytelling How to Draw Readers Into the Page

Storytelling – this very basic art form is a powerful way to build rapport between you and your customer.

Whether you are creating a story to describe your product or you are telling customers the story of your life, you will find that stories are effective because they stick in the mind for much longer than facts and figures do.

Have you ever zoned out during a business meeting that focuses on, say, the first quarter sales numbers and how they compare and contrast to previous years. Yuck.

Your brain isn't engaged, and you probably are going to have to refer back to those numbers again and again because they just won't stick in the brain.

Stories work because they engage all of your senses. You can empathize, focus on details, and imagine textures and sounds. You connect with the storyteller on an emotional level.

If the leaders of your business meeting had woven a story into their presentation of facts and figures, you would have probably been able to pay a lot closer attention to the content.

Storytelling as a Lifestyle

Pottery Barn and Restoration Hardware have learned that selling a lifestyle is almost as important as selling a product. Take a look at the product descriptions on their Web sites. They focus on rich, textural details that speak to the person you want to be rather than the person you are.

This can be a very important selling tool. You can use storytelling to show customers what their lives can be like if they only purchase your product.

Storytelling as a Motivational Tool

Consider telling your story – your business background, your ideals and values, your core beliefs.

By sharing this information with your customers, you are communicating who you are and allowing your customers to connect to you.

You might think, why would anyone want to hear the personal details of my life? Well, have you ever been asked, "Tell me a little bit about yourself"? Of course you have.

People are genuinely interested in people, and by sharing this information, you are helping to build a closer relationship between you and your customers.

Also, this is a perfect opportunity to showcase yourself as a wise guru. Your decisions and actions have made you what you are today. By illustrating that, you are showing customers that they can trust your judgment and counsel.

Another way to do this is to take a look at your resume and your business accomplishments. Craft little stories from resume points – highlighting how you solved problems, came up with cost-cutting measures, etc.

Storytelling as a Method of Showcasing Success Highlighting success stories is one of the most basic uses for this marketing technique. A short success story can illustrate a point, serve as a testimonial, or reinforce a sales point.

Take a moment and talk with some of your customers. Ask how your product has helped them 30, 60, or 90 days later. Turn that into a short story that you can use to draw people into your Web site.

Show a before and after, reveal what the secret to success was. Readers love to hear stories that illustrate measurable growth, and they also love to hear "secrets" that will help them be successful.

The Basics of Storytelling

- Don't be afraid to use dramatic license. Don't lie, but feel free to pump up the drama.
- Create a sense of urgency. Make the reader feel like time is of the essence in your story.
- Use vivid words that convey emotions.
- Don't use jargon and overwhelm your readers with a lot of facts. Keep it simple.

Chapter 4: Basic Copywriting Pulling It All Together

Now that we've gone through the background you need to create your sales page – target audience, your unique selling position, and how to use stories to engage an audience – we can move onto the basics of copywriting.

Several basic copywriting elements are common to almost every ad.

Headline: The headline is usually the biggest typographical element on the page. It's supposed to be the "entry point" into the ad. It's an attention- grabber.

It should also be simple enough to get your point across in a limited space. You don't want your headline to be too long or complex.

Focus on a core problem or a key benefit of what you are offering. People are five times more likely to read a headline than to delve into body copy.

I give you examples of headlines in Chapter 7 and 8.

Subhead: This reinforces the headline or re-states the headline in a different way. Let your reader know that this is the ad they need to read. They need to know right up front that this is the place they want to be.

Think of newspapers when you are writing your headline and subheads. In any good newspaper, you should be able to scan the headlines and subheads of page one and know most of the news right away. The rest of the stories are just details.

In the following examples, the format will be HEADLINE: SUBHEAD.

Example

- Seven Ways to Make Money on the Internet: Yours Free With a Purchase

- How to Get the Most Out of Your Search Engine Ads: The Top Secrets Marketers Don't Want You to Know

Body Copy: This starts with a lead paragraph that offers you the meat of the ad. There are several techniques that you can use to draw the reader into the copy.

Try opening with a question or by extending an offer. You can also try opening with a story, but be sure that there is a phrase in the first couple of sentences that gives the reader your pitch and tells them why this product will change their life.

Subsequent paragraphs both illustrate and reinforce your main selling points.

The final paragraph offers a "call to action" such as "Click here to purchase this fantastic offer." You must ALWAYS have a call to action.

Then, add a PS at the end of the page that restates the offer and gives customers a reason to respond to the offer. This is a very common technique used in direct mail marketing. Research has shown that most people will skip down to the PS to see what the offer is. You might want to offer an exciting guarantee that your customer can't possibly refuse.

This structure is used for almost every kind of direct response letter.

Things to remember

Research has also shown that people are six times more likely to read an editorial article than an advertisement. What does this mean for your writing?

You should focus on writing copy so that it feels like an editorial article.

27

The average American consumer is bombarded by advertisements - up to one or two thousand per day. So in order to grab your reader's attention, you need to make your copy stand out.

Also, play to the reader's emotions. There's a reason that small items like candy or gum or magazines are at the checkout counter in grocery stores. They are called impulse buys - customers feel a particular emotion and purchase something on an impulse. You can do the same thing with your copy, by causing them to have an emotional reaction to your product.

Another tip is to make sure that the copy comes from a first-person perspective of the consumer. Use "you" and "your". Make it personal. But be sure not to use the imperial "we" in your copy. Say "you'll love this product" instead of "we have the best product."

Internal repetition can be very important. Don't be afraid to state, and re-state, your offer in a variety of different ways.

And finally, make sure that you try to communicate credibility. Think to your own buying habits. Aren't you more likely to purchase something from a company that has a lot of credibility in the marketplace? Maybe they've been in business for 50 years, or have great word-of-mouth. Usually there is something that attracts you, as a consumer, to their site.

Whatever makes you credible – be it experience or length of time in business or whatever – make sure that's loud and clear to your readers.

You can offer testimonials from real people (printing their full name) as a measure of establishing credibility. You can offer specific numbers instead of estimations.

Be sure to mention any favorable third-party reviews you have received. ("Voted best customer service by the users of www.website.com!") And if you have credentials or awards that you have won relating to the product, just say so. All of these things will help you establish credibility with your customers.

The Web vs. Direct Mail

Many of the same writing techniques found in direct mail can be used on the Web as well. However, there are a few things you should consider.

Eye-tracking studies have shown that almost 80% of people scan the web, as opposed to reading every word. This means that you have to concentrate on writing copy that can be scanned easily. Include lots of headlines and subheads. Don't cram your paragraphs and words together – make sure there's plenty of white space.

And above all, use short and simple sentences. You shouldn't be afraid of making your Web page long enough to tell your story, but within that context, make your copy simple and your paragraphs short. Always write to the lowest common denominator, because you can never assume that your readers will be well-educated.

When writing for the Web, you should use bullets as much as possible, because they are easy to scan. You can itemize all of your benefits and put them in order of importance. Or illustrate the steps in the buying process with a numbered list.

A couple more sales tricks include using a bold guarantee and a valuable bonus. The bold guarantee is simply a block of text that stands out from regular copy and offers a refund if not fully delighted, exclusive money-back offer, etc.

The valuable bonus is something that you throw in as an incentive. Often, people will purchase something just to get the valuable bonus. ("Buy a Dell Dimension desktop PC and get an HP printer for free!") The bonus doesn't have to be costly to you, but it should be something that's valuable to the customer. Free samples, startup guides, and tutorials are all valuable bonuses that have great value.

The Don'ts

Don't get so caught up in your story that you lose sight of your main goal – to make sales. Don't bury your message; hammer it home again and again.

Don't rely on spin over substance. If your page has too many "amazing" and "wonderful" and "fantastic" descriptions, your reader is going to start realizing that your site has too many empty words – and that will destroy your credibility.

Don't stretch the truth. Readers can spot a lie a mile away.

Don't forget about specifics. If you can say that you made more than $1,000 profit the first week, then say so. Specifics are more impressive than generalities.

Don't meander. Your stories should have a beginning, middle and end. Keep the readers moving to the call to action.

Don't offend people. Seriously. Don't include that questionable joke, don't make that stereotype, and don't criticize your competitor. Don't do anything that will drive the reader away.

Don't forget to proofread. Make liberal use of the spelling and grammar checker, because the quickest way to lose your credibility with an audience is to have an ad that's filled with spelling errors.

Don't forget to ask for the order. Make a link that says "Order Now" or something similar.

Don't forget to sum up. Your final paragraph should sum up all of your most important sales points. Then, you can add the call to action.

Chapter 5: Features vs. Benefits

Experienced copywriters know that it's better to highlight the benefits of a product, rather than its features. Why? Again, it's because benefits offer an answer to the question, "What's in it for me?"

An example: Dell laptop computers contain wireless technology.

Wireless technology is a popular feature of computers. However, you can't always assume that your customers will know what wireless technology is and why that will benefit them.

So when writing about wireless technology as a benefit, you would say something like, "Wireless technology allows you to connect to the Internet anywhere you wish – such as airports, coffee shops, and anywhere you find yourself doing business."

So, a feature is a factual statement about a product. But a benefit offers the customer something of value, thereby making it more attractive.

When you are trying to sell a product using only the features, you are making the customer do all the work to figure out how the product will fit into his or her lifestyle. It's in your best interest to do the work for the customer.

Chapter 6: Words That Sell

What do you think is the most important word in advertising? Money? Easy? Free?

In reality, the most important word is "you." Your customers want to feel important – like you are talking to them directly, on a personal level.

Instead of writing, "My clients have experienced XX with this product," you would write, "You will experience XX with this product." Remember, this is another way to see things from a client's perspective.

Now, those other words – money, easy, and free – are also great words that sell.

Money, for instance. People love a good bargain. So if your product will save your customers money in the long run, make this one of your main selling points. And remember to be specific. I will be more intrigued by a product that promises to save me $1,000 over a product that promises to save me "lots of money."

Easy is also a good selling word. Everyone has busy work schedules and lives. No one wants to purchase something that's going to make another demand on their time. So if you can highlight the easy ways a product can fit into someone's lifestyle, or how easy it is to order the product, you will see sales go up exponentially.

And, if money and easy aren't enough, just throw in something for free. Customers love to get something for nothing, and free is one of the top sales words. Just take a look into your spam mailbox, for example. See how many of the offers have the word free in the subject line.

Three More Great Words

Try yes, benefit and using a person's first name. First off, yes.

People love to hear the word yes. And this is a really easy thing to incorporate into copy. Ask a series of yes/no questions, and at the end, write, "If you answered yes to any of these questions …" See how easy that is?

Now, the word benefit. We have talked about benefits, but not necessarily using the actual word. Don't be afraid to talk about the "added benefits" or talk about how a customer can "reap the benefits."

And don't forget the power of a person's name. This is another way to bring your copy to a personal level. If you are making a personal presentation, or sending a marketing letter, include the first name of your prospect.

More Words That Sell

- Amazing
- Announcing
- Bargain
- Best
- Bonus
- Breakthrough
- Challenge
- Compare
- Discount
- Discover
- Easy
- Free
- Fun
- Genuine
- Gift
- Guarantee
- Health
- How-to
- Hurry
- Improvement
- Introducing
- Last chance
- Love

- Magic
- Miracle
- Money
- More
- New
- No – no obligation, no risk guarantee, etc.
- Now
- Offer
- Opportunity
- Proven
- Quick
- Remarkable
- Results
- Revolutionary
- Save
- Sensational
- Simple
- Solution
- Special
- Startling
- Success
- Suddenly
- Unique

- Value
- Wanted

And here are words broken down into categories that will fit the different headline types we'll discuss in the next chapter.

Words That Convey News

- Announcing
- Introducing
- Latest
- Modern
- New
- Novel
- Now
- Presenting
- Recent
- Revolutionary
- Suddenly
- Today

Words That Convey Value

- Accepted
- Acclaimed

- Admired
- Approved
- Authorized
- Certified
- Commended
- Complimented
- Endorsed
- Guaranteed
- Honored
- Lauded
- Popular
- Praised
- Proven
- Recognized
- Recommended
- Sanctioned
- Tested

Words That Convey Surprise

- Amazing
- Astonishing
- Astounding
- Exceptional
- Extraordinary

- Fantastic
- Magic
- Miracle
- Notable
- Noteworthy
- Remarkable
- Sensational
- Singular
- Startling
- Strange
- Striking
- Stunning
- Surprising
- Uncommon
- Unusual

Words That Convey Quality

- Authentic
- Better
- Choice
- Durable
- Excellent
- Exclusive
- Famous

- Fine
- First-Rate
- Genuine
- Good
- Greatest
- Imported
- Improved
- Limited
- Noted
- Outstanding
- Personalized
- Rare
- Remarkable
- Rugged
- Selected
- Special
- Superior
- Surpassing
- Terrific
- Top
- Unique
- Unparalleled
- Unsurpassed
- Valuable

- Wonderful

Words for Money Headlines

- Abundance
- Affluence
- Bounty
- Fortune
- Liberal
- Luxury
- Profitable
- Prosperity
- Prosperous
- Resources
- Revenue
- Riches
- Wealth

Reference Books

For more examples of words that sell, many copywriters recommend the following books:

"Words That Sell: The Thesaurus to Help You Promote Your Products,

Services, and Ideas" by Richard Bayan

"More Words That Sell" by Richard Bayan

"Phrases That Sell: The Ultimate Phrase Finder to Help You Promote Your Products, Services, and Ideas" by Edward Werz and Sally Germain

"Persuasive Online Copywriting: How to Take Your Words to the Bank" by Bryan Eisenberg

Chapter 7: Breaking Down the Headline

A lot of companies have conducted what is called "eye- tracking" research. They use machines to track how an eye moves down the printed page or a web page.

Contrary to what most people believe, researchers have found through this technology that consumers look at text before they look at images. A snappy headline that is dominant (the biggest thing) on the page draws the eye first. So a headline isn't just filler copy; it's the single most important thing on your sales page.

The whole purpose of a catchy headline is to grab the reader's attention and make the reader want to purchase in order to learn more. So when writing headlines, the top three things to remember are: to convey a benefit or a selling point, use 15 words or less, and make sure that the headline can stand on its own.

First, conveying a benefit. You want to make sure that your headline clearly promises a benefit. This is yet another call-back to the idea that a reader wants to know, "What's in it for me?"

Second, you want to make this statement in 15 words or less. Any longer and you no longer have a headline, you have a paragraph. In fact, the fewer words, the better.

Finally, a headline needs to stand on its own. Remember a while back, when I suggested scanning the front page of a newspaper? Those headlines could stand on their own, if need be. Most newspapers have headlines that convey the essential parts of a story.

A great headline trick is to use numbers, because people respond to numbers and lists. Take a look at some women's magazines. What headlines will you see on the cover?

"10 Ways to Get a Man."

"12 Secrets to Success."

"50 Great Looks for Summer."

All of these headlines are meant to get people to open the magazine and purchase it to read more. The implied benefits are, you will get a man, be successful or look good this summer. And all in six words or less.

The 9 Types of Headlines

Nine types of headlines are typically used in the copywriting world:

1. Headlines That Offer a Benefit

With this type of headline, you really have to know your target audience. Research what triggers them to buy, what their "hot buttons" are. Then create a headline that offers that benefit in a creative way.

Say the benefit of your product is that it will help the buyer make money faster. Here's a headline that will offer that benefit: Make Money Faster With This New Referral System.

Examples:

- Amazing Secrets That Add Money to Your Pocket.
- Read This Now, Or Kiss Your Money Goodbye.
- Triple Your Response With This Ad.

2. The Personalized Headline

This type of headline is a really good one. Have you ever opened up a Publisher's Clearinghouse letter? Have you noticed that they always refer to you by your first and last name? The personalized headline is any type of headline that also includes the customer's name.

Personalized headlines make sales letters seem less like form letters and more like letters that were created especially for you. By giving the appearance of a personal relationship, you will get people interested who wouldn't normally respond to your ad.

Examples:

- Amazing Secrets That Add Money to Your Pocket
- How You, Mary, Can Make Money in Your Sleep

3. The Testimonial Headline

When you combine a headline and a testimonial, you get an endorsement that has quite an impact. Talk to some of your customer's about the benefits they've received from your product, and craft that into a short, powerful testimonial headline.

Examples:

- How I Retired After Only 7 Months in Business
- I Lost 50 Pounds, and You Can Too
- I've Saved 37% Since Using This System
- How I Made a Fortune With a Crazy Idea

4. **The Guarantee Headline**

This headline promises a desirable benefit to the reader. This type of headline increases trust with the reader. After all, in order to guarantee something, you must believe in the product. You can guarantee a refund, or results, or some other benefit.

Examples:

- Play the Guitar in 7 Days or Your Money Back
- Increase Your Leads by 40%, Guaranteed!

5. **The Discount Sale Headline**

The discount sales headline is a compelling, act- now headline. This is the best format for announcing a limited sales event or discount. You can make this kind of headline even more compelling by adding a "reason why." Tell the reader why you're offering the discount.

Examples:

- I Want to Help You Succeed: Save 10% in June.
- We're Overstocked, So I'm Passing the Savings On to You.

6. The News Headline

The most basic headline offers something that's newsworthy. This is especially a good headline for major company changes or hot new products.

Examples:

- This Just In: 10 Ad Secrets That Could Change Your Life.

- Announcing a Brand-New Lead Generation System That's Perfect for You.
- At Last, the Perfect Weight-Loss System.

7. **The How-To Headline**

People like to learn. If you have a system that shows people how to do something, use a how-to headline.

Examples:

- How to Test a Winning Sales Process
- How to Become a Web Millionaire
- How to Profit From the 7 Secrets They Don't Want You to Know

8. **Headlines That Offer a Solution**

This headline takes your target market's biggest problem or frustration and offers a solution to the problem.

Examples:

If You Were to Lose Your Job Tomorrow, Would You Be Prepared? Here's a Guaranteed Way to Make Sure This Won't Happen to You.

9. **Headlines That Ask a Question**

Before using this headline, you have to make sure your KNOW what motivates your target market.

Examples:

- How Much Money Do You Really Want to Make in Your Business?
- What's Your Best Chance to Succeed? The Answer May Surprise You

Chapter 8: Creating Snappy Headlines

Weekly gossip magazines are great places to find examples of snappy headlines. Because of space limitations, their headline writers have learned to convey a lot of meaning into just a few phrases.

For example, look at the National Enquirer. You will see an image of the cover of this week's paper, as well as headlines of top stories from the Web site.

Nick and Jessica: Finally Over.

Stedman Betrays Oprah with a Tell-All Book.

Keira: I'm Not Anorexic.

Nicole and Keith Marry!

Now, of course you need to know a little bit about the celebrity world to understand who they are talking about. But the Enquirer definitely knows their audience, and the headline writers know that readers will instantly know the meaning of these headlines:

Nick and Jessica: Finally Over — Nick Lachey and Jessica Simpson are divorced.

Stedman Betrays Oprah with a Tell-All Book — Oprah Winfrey's boyfriend has spilled her secrets.

Keira: I'm Not Anorexic — Keira Knightley says her thinness isn't because of an eating disorder.

Nicole and Keith Marry! — Nicole Kidman and Keith Richards have married.

Those headlines are very short and self-explanatory, but they aren't very snappy. For that, we turn to the world of daily tabloid newspapers.

Tabloid newspapers, which were started in London and have gradually drifted over to the U.S., have made an art out of the snappy headline. Because they are smaller in size to regular broadsheet newspapers, headline writers also have to pack a lot of punch into a few words.

Try the New York Post, London's Daily Mirror, and New York's Newsday.

Some examples from the Daily Mirror:

How Can 59,017,382 People Be So Dumb? — perfectly illustrates Britain's reaction to the re-election of President Bush, as he is not popular there.

Careless Spliffer: George Michael's Cannabis Arrest — a really great two-word headline that plays on the George Michael song "Careless Whisper" and a spliff, which is a nickname for a marijuana cigarette.

The following headlines are also two-worders. The main headline is large, the biggest thing on the page, followed by an explanatory subhead.

Some examples from the New York Post:

Jack Owe: Star's Cash Meltdown – a great play on Michael Jackson's nickname Jacko.

Bling Sting: 'Jacob the Jeweler' in drug-$$ bust – Jacob the Jeweler practically invented "bling," the rapper's trend of wearing flashy jewelry with tons of diamonds. He was arrested in a drug sting.

Hurri-Con: $1.4 billion in Katrina aid bought sex & booze – another absolutely great two-worder, a mashup of "hurricane" and "con," referring to how FEMA money from Hurricane Katrina was misspent in 2005.

Applying the Message

Now that you're inspired, let's take a look at advertising

headlines that have been proven to sell.

- Are You Frustrated With the Money You've Been Making?

- How to Put an End to Prospecting While You Earn a Six-Figure Income.

- Your Employer Doesn't Want You to Read This Ad.

- Where the Money is and How to Get It.

- We're Looking for People Who Want to Make Money.

- Too Busy Earning a Living to Make Any Money?

- The Secret of Being Wealthy.

- The Quickest Way I Know to Make a Million Dollars

Do you see why these are successful? They speak to something that appeals to most people – we all wish we could be making more money than we do currently. Don't you want to click on one to see what the secret is?

Create a Headline Swipe File

As you are browsing the newspaper, a magazine, or the Internet, remember to keep a file of useful phrases that you can use in the future. This is called a headline "swipe file."

You can borrow any kind of headline and make it your own very quickly. All you have to do is replace certain words in the original headline with the words or phrases that will help you sell your product.

For example:

The Secret to Becoming a Millionaire is Simply Using the Right Words!

The Secret to _____is Simply_____!

What could you plug into those spaces that would work for your product?

The Secret to Losing Weight is Simply the Johnson Diet!

The Secret to Making Money on the Web is Simply to Write Copy That Sells!

The Secret to Marketing is Simply to Know Your Audience!

Why create a headline swipe file? Well, in reality, you should have a swipe file of headlines, letters, salutations, postscripts, etc.

There's no sense in reinventing the wheel every time you need a new sales letter.

You should have some boilerplate explanatory copy that you use in each letter, and you should have swipe files containing ideas for you to use. This will save you time in the long run.

Here are some more headlines that you can use to kick off your swipe file:

The Only Two Ways to Super Wealth and How to Join the Wealthy Elite.

The Only Two Ways to_____ Elite and How to Join the_____

The 10 Wackiest Ideas That Made Millions, and How You Can Too.

The 10 Wackiest Ideas That _____, and How You Can Too.

Stop Dreaming and Start Making Money

Stop _____ and Start_____.

Sick and Tired of Making Your Boss Rich?

Sick and Tired of _____?

Remember When You Could Have Picked Up a Great Piece of Real Estate for a Song and You Didn't?

Remember When You Could Have _____ and You _____Didn't?

The Day-to-Day Grind Got You Down? We've Got the Solution!

The _____Solution! Got You Down? We've Got the _____

Just Released ... 19 of the World's Top Marketing Geniuses Reveal Little Known Marketing Secrets That Could Make You Rich!

Just Released _____ of the World's
Top Marketing Geniuses Reveal
Little Known _____ Secrets That
Could Make You Rich!

**How to Write Headlines That Will
Make You Rich.**

How to _____That Will Make You
Rich.

**How to Use Library Books to Boost
Your Sales.**

How to Use _____to Boost Your
Sales.

**How to Turn Your Kitchen Into a
Well-Oiled Profit- Making Machine.**

How to Turn _____ Into a Well-
Oiled, Profit-Making Machine.

How to Turn Obstacles Into Opportunities.

How to Turn _____ Into _____.

How to Turn $45 Into $483,000.00 in Just 1 Year.

How to Turn _____Into _____in Just _____

How to Take the Headache Out of Writing.

How to Take the Headache Out of _____

How to Start With Nothing and Create a Money-Making Empire.

How to Start With _____and Create a _____.

How to Make People Line Up and Beg to Give You Money.

How to Make People Line Up and Beg to _____

How to Get Rich in Today's Economy.

How to _____ in Today's Economy.

The Complete Do-It-Yourself Guide to Personal and Financial Survival.

The Complete Do-It-Yourself Guide to _____

How to Double Your Business in Six Months -- 100% Guaranteed!!!

How to Double _____ in _____ Months 100% Guaranteed!!!

Hidden Profits in Your Computer.

Hidden _____ in Your _____

Here's the Quickest & Easiest Way for You to Succeed in Mail Order.

Here's the Quickest & Easiest Way for You to Succeed in _____

Get Paid $20,000 for Each Book You Read.

Get Paid _____ for _____

Get Out of Debt Without Borrowing.

Get _____ Without _____

Do You Honestly Want to Be Rich?

Do You Honestly Want to _____

Some More Useful Phrases That You Can Build a Headline Around

Announcing Bargain Free!
Be Your Own Boss
The Secret of ... Advice

68

Facts
Last Minute
Save
Amazing Sensational Revolutionary
Finally
At Last
New Breakthrough
How to …
Own Your Own …
I Discovered How to …
I'm Revealing the Secret to … The
Truth About …

Chapter 9: Test, Test, Test

One of the most important things to consider with your marketing is testing. This is especially true with headlines, because one headline might not hit the mark.

Most good marketers know that you have to sometimes test 3 or 4 headlines before determining which one works the best.

Let's use some of the examples in chapter 7 as an example.

The Secret to Making Money on the Web is Simply to Write Copy That Sells!

The Secret to Marketing is Simply to Know Your Audience!

Now, I would use the first headline for a week, measure my traffic and count how many leads I gathered with this headline.

Then, I would put the second headline up for a week. Do the same measurements and compare the two headlines.

Did one get you more traffic than the other? Did one gather more leads for you? Or you could put two sales letters up and test both headlines simultaneously.

The purpose of testing is to make sure that you are using the headlines that will generate the most response. A small change in a headline can have a dramatic difference in response rates.

Chapter 10: The Importance of Incentives

As we discussed a little bit in Chapter 4, incentives (or "a valuable bonus") are important things that can convert a reader from a prospect into a customer.

By including a bonus or incentive to your offer, you are giving your customer the perception that they are receiving great value for their money.

If possible, the value of the incentive should come close to the actual price of the main product. That way, your customers will feel as if they have gotten a great bargain. In fact, in many cases a customer will purchase because they want the incentive and not necessarily the main product.

Make sure, however, that the bonus is useful and relevant to the actual product. You can consider including extra features for free or providing valuable information, such as a tutorial or research paper.

Chapter 11: Offering Customer Testimonials

Customer testimonials can go a long way towards helping you establish credibility and overcoming skepticism on the part of the prospect. With any kind of advertising, there is a degree of skepticism; consumers know when they are being "sold". But when a third-party with nothing to gain starts singing your praises, it becomes clear that you are a merchant that is trustworthy.

Testimonials help break down objections that a customer might have to a product. Take a look at some of those late-night infomercials, for example. They are littered with testimonials from satisfied customers. And why? Because they work.

Some believe that is because people automatically respond to what other people do. Remember that old phrase, if your best friend jumped off a cliff, would you? That's also true with sales. If your best friend buys a product and they rave about it, you will probably want to try the product too. So a customer testimonial is just like having your best friend talk about your product.

Learning About Loyalty

It has been said that customers who are willing to give testimonials are more loyal to your brand and your product. Once people have publicly stated that they endorse a certain company, they tend to stand by that decision. So this added bonus means that if a customer gives you a testimonial, you know you just might have a customer for life.

Getting a Successful Testimonial

The easiest way to get a testimonial is to ask for comments

and feedback. But that isn't necessarily the best testimonial for your product. You want to have powerful thoughts that will catch a new customer's attention. So consider using these tips to solicit a testimonial.

1. Ask for a testimonial within a few days of the sale. This is when your customer will still be excited about their purchase and when they will be most likely to give you some help.

2. Ask for the testimonial to speak to a specific aspect of the sales transaction. If one of your sales points is customer service, ask your customer to comment on that particular thing.

3. Ask the customer to talk about how they have benefited from the product. Did they struggle before they received it? Did it solve an issue for them?

4. Is your customer an expert in the field? Make sure that they include their credentials. This will make your product seem more credible, as people automatically look up to authority figures.

5. Try and get a picture of the customer. This is just a little thing that makes the testimonial come to life and enhances the believability factor.

Once you've gotten a testimonial from a customer, don't forget to get permission to use it in an advertisement. That way, your bases are covered.

Chapter 12: How to Format Your Sales Page

When formatting your page, you want to make sure that you can interest two kinds of customers - those who are analytical and want to read lengthy copy that gives as much detail as possible, and those who are impulsive and just want to get to the meat of the offer quickly.

To do this, you should make sure to write long copy with lots of details, and then pepper it with headlines, subheads, info boxes, etc. that can be easily skimmed and still offer a point.

We've already talked about how to create a snappy headline. But you should also make sure that the headline is bold and one of the biggest - if not the biggest - thing on the page.

Subheads can be the same size as the body copy, but make them bold or a different color. You can also make them one or two points bigger, in order to make them stand out.

You can break up the copy with the use of pull quotes – a sentence that's pulled out of a paragraph and set off in a different typeface. And you can also add definition and white space by using bulleted points or numbered lists.

The most important thing, however, is to be consistent. Don't have some headlines in one font and size and others in a different font and size. Consistency creates a look-and-feel that works from page to page and helps readers stay visually oriented and comfortable.

You'll find some formatting examples on the next page.

EXAMPLE HEADLINE

SUBHEAD – same font but smaller and different color

First paragraph of body copy that's going to pull the reader into the rest of the story. First paragraph of body copy that's going to pull the reader into the rest of the story.

Another paragraph. Notice how short and sweet my sentences are? See how few sentences can fit into a paragraph?

It's time for a subhead

And some more body copy. Now I'm going to put placeholder text in the copy for the rest of the page. This is what designers call "greek text."

Lorem ipsum dolor sit amet, consectetuer adipiscing elit. Nullam eleifend arcu vitae odio. Morbi posuere.

Donec nisl augue, fringilla sed, gravida id, consequat sed, enim. Suspendisse potenti. Quisque ipsum tellus, tempus vel, rhoncus eget, rhoncus at, felis.

Another subhead

Lorem ipsum dolor sit amet, consectetuer adipiscing elit. Nullam eleifend arcu vitae odio. Morbi posuere.

Here's a list of my sales points:

- Most important

- Second most important

- Third most important

- Etc.

- And etc.

- And etc.

Another subhead

Lorem ipsum dolor sit amet, consectetuer adipiscing elit. Nullam eleifend arcu vitae odio. Morbi posuere.

Here's a pull quote. Maybe it's part of a testimonial:

"Donec nisl augue, fringilla sed, gravida id, consequat sed, enim."

--- person's name

"Donec nisl augue, fringilla sed, gravida id, consequat sed, enim."

--- person's name

And here we go back to your body copy. Nullam eleifend arcu vitae odio. Morbi posuere.

And a numbered list with certain words emphasized:

1. Like **this**, and *this* and <u>this</u>

2. But don't forget **this** and *this*

3. And **this**, and *this* and **this**

4. And **that** and **that** as well

Now we've got some more copy to talk about. Lorem ipsum dolor sit amet, consectetuer adipiscing elit. Nullam eleifend arcu vitae odio. Morbi posuere.

Lorem ipsum dolor sit amet, consectetuer adipiscing elit. Nullam eleifend arcu vitae odio. Morbi posuere.

And we're finally wrapping things up. Don't forget to give your call to action right here. In fact, you can give a bold-faced guarantee right before you sign off.

Your signature,

PS. Don't forget to restate the offer with a PS!

Chapter 13: Killer Sales Letter Secrets

Finally, here are some little secrets that will help you become a successful copywriter.

Message to Market Match

Don't forget that your message absolutely has to match what your market is thinking.

That's right. You have to imagine yourself into your consumer's mindset. What motivates them? What is important to them.

Copywriting is a lot like psychology. It's about human behavior. It's not about selling. It's about figuring out what will trigger your consumer to BUY.

Be Clear in Your Message

This point is pretty simple. You want to make sure you are writing to the lowest common denominator.

You don't have to use a lot of 50-cent words to make your point. In fact, the more clear in language you can be, and the more precise, the easier your copy will be to read.

Don't Make Your Ad Look Like an Ad

We are bombarded with advertising messages every day. Think about how many billboards you see on your way to work, how many ads on the radio you hear, how many banners on the Internet you see, and how many ads you see at night on TV.

Consumers are tired of the ad attack. The less your ad looks like an ad and the more it looks like a testimonial or story, the more people will read it and the more consumers will purchase.

More Headline Tips

- Never use all uppercase letters in your headline. On the Internet, that's considered shouting. Plus, it's very hard to read.

- "Quote marks around a headline improve response."

- Don't fix what isn't broken. If something works and you don't know why, don't question. Just keep using it.

- When testing, only switch the headline.

- Use your best stuff first, at the top of the letter.

- In your body copy, write as you talk.

- Restate your headline and call to action in the PS.

- Answer all their objections in the copy.

Other books that I have also authored and are available in kindle, paperback and audio are the following:

How To Create A Profitable Ezine From Scratch

The Secrets Of Making $10,000 on Ebay in 30 Days

The Complete Guide To Investing in Gold And Silver: Surviving The Great Economic Depression

How To Make A Fortune Using The Public Domain

Search Engine Domination: The Ultimate Secrets To Increasing Your Website's Visibility And Making A Ton Of Cash

Creative Real Estate Investing Strategies And Tips

How to Overcome Your Self-Limiting Beliefs & Achieve Anything You Want

The Secrets of Finding The Perfect Ghostwriter For Your Book

The Creative Real Estate Marketing Equation: Motivated Sellers + Motivated Buyers = $

How To Start An Online Business With Less Than $200

How To Market Your Business Online and Offline

Audiobook Profits: How To Make Money by Turning Your Kindle, Paperback, And Hard cover Book Into Audio

How To Make Money Online: The Savvy Entrepreneurs Guide To Financial Freedom

The Fine Art of Writing The Next Best Seller On Kindle

How To Promote Market And Sell Your Kindle Book